REST LIGHTLY

AN ANTHOLOGY OF
LATIN AND GREEK TOMB INSCRIPTIONS

Translated by

PAUL SHORE

BOLCHAZY-CARDUCCI PUBLISHERS, INC.
Wauconda, Illinois USA

General Editor:
Gaby Huebner

Contributing Editor:
Laurie Haight Keenan

Cover Illustration:
"Severina nutrix"
Tombstone from the second half of the third century.
RGM, Cologne, Germany, no. 331 (see p. 14)

Typeset, Layout and Cover Design:
Charlene M. Hernandez

BOLCHAZY-CARDUCCI PUBLISHERS, INC.
1000 Brown Street
Wauconda, Illinois 60084 USA

http://www.bolchazy.com

ISBN 0-86516-355-3

Printed in the United States of America
2000
by United Graphics

Library of Congress Cataloging-in-Publication Data

Rest lightly : an anthology of Latin and Greek tomb inscriptions /
translated by Paul Shore.
      p.   cm.
   ISBN 0–86516–355–3 (pbk. : alk. paper)
   1. Inscriptions, Latin   2. Inscriptions, Greek.   3. Epitaphs.
I. Shore, Paul J., 1956–   .
CN528.E6R47 1997
929'.5'0072—dc21   97–19130
                                                 CIP

FOR ILENE

UXORI OPTIMAE

COMITI IN VIA VITAE

PREFACE

Using tombstone inscriptions to interest school age students in the ancient world and to teach them about it in a significant way may seem *prima facie* to be a difficult undertaking (no pun intended!). After all, what can be deader (or more morbid, duller, or more intrinsically "uncool") than a tombstone inscription, except perhaps if it is composed in a "dead" language such as Latin or ancient Greek?

The truth is that tomb inscriptions offer insights into the ancient people that are rarely available from other sources and, as any teacher who has tried using inscriptions in the classroom knows, inscriptions manage to grab the attention of teenagers and pre-teenagers alike. Their very strangeness, newness, and off-beat character as well as their frequent beauty stimulate interest and command attention.

The present anthology makes available in convenient and attractive format about 30 engaging and well-selected tomb inscriptions culled from a wide variety of sources. Inscriptional texts appear in the classical languages and in readable, fresh English translations. Photographs of tombstones as well as appropriate annotations are included.

This material could be used in a various ways:

✦ Latin teachers could use it in whole or in part as the basis of a unit or mini-unit or as supplementary reading for pupils. The texts could be read, explicated, and discussed in class the way other Latin literature is. Pupils could be asked to react to the texts in writing or orally in class. Since translations are provided, the anthology could be used at almost any level of Latin study from upper elementary school through high school.

✦ Teachers of ancient history or world history could use the inscriptions to illustrate aspects of ancient private life and to put students in direct contact with the words and thoughts of ancient people, especially "ordinary" people including often neglected groups such as women and children.

✦ Teachers of world literature could incorporate individual inscriptions into literature units dealing with loss and death and to compare and contrast ancient and modern attitudes and viewpoints. Individual inscriptions could also serve as source materials in the study of aspects of classical mythology.

v

◆ Homeschoolers and autodidacts could use the anthology in whole or in part as a valuable resource for individualized independent study projects.

Paul Shore and Bolchazy-Carducci Publishers deserve our gratitude for making such rich educational fare available.

DR. RUDOLPH MASCIANTONIO
Director of Foreign Language Education Emeritus
The School District of Philadelphia

ACKNOWLEDGMENTS

The translator wishes to acknowledge the assistance of Professors Olin Storvik and Edith Kovach, who helped in the translation of the inscriptions. Lola Mae Philippsen provided valuable assistance in tracking down the originals of many inscriptions, and Professor Charlotte Iiams gave useful suggestions on the readability of the translations. In the final preparation of the manuscript, Lynn Timmons, Liz Janz, Colleen O'Sullivan, Dawnella Rose, and Christine Hoester provided tireless and intelligent assistance. Merri Jean Manetzke assisted in formatting. I also wish to thank Gaby Huebner and Laurie Haight of Bolchazy-Carducci Publishers for their assistance in the final editing of the manuscript, and Charlene Hernandez of Bolchazy-Carducci Publishers for professionalizing the layout.

All illustrations appear with the kind permission of the Römisch-Germanisches Museum, Cologne.

This project was funded in part by the Moorhead State University Foundation.

"A Roman Matron's Epitaph" appeared in slightly different form in *Red Weather*. "A Nonbeliever's Tomb" and "On the Death of a Little Girl" appeared in slightly different form in *Encounters, Estrangements, Connections.*

CONTENTS

INTRODUCTION

I
The Value of Tomb Inscriptions

Millions of individuals lived during the centuries in which Rome dominated the Mediterranean, and the overwhelming majority left no trace of their existence behind. Although we know a great deal about the Roman world in comparison with other ancient civilizations, our knowledge is skewed by social inequalities, chance, and the bias of later writers and historians. The random event of a natural disaster allows the modern researcher to gain glimpses of everyday life in Pompeii and Herculaneum rather than that of Palmyra or Vindobona (Vienna). Our understanding of the major figures in Roman history is further supported by a web of research in fields as diverse as numismatics, architecture, and paleography.

But when all the evidence available is sifted and interpreted, huge gaps remain. The literary sources, which continue to be the most important source for information about the lives of individuals, have been winnowed for centuries by chance destruction, such as the fires in the Alexandrian library in 391 and 642 C.E., and by the deliberate editing and censoring of anonymous scribes. Not only are the documents that have survived a biased sample, but the circumstances that created the bias often make it impossible to determine what is missing in our knowledge of noted individuals. In a broader sense, however, some lacunae are very obvious. Classical Latin and Greek literature to a large extent ignores women and children. Culturally, the focus of much of the literary record is on the patrician class. Slaves, the urban proletariat, and small farmers receive only peripheral attention as individuals in the *Satires* of Juvenal and other works describing Roman life. Like many other societies, Rome lavished resources and effort on the preservation of an elitist view of individuals and their contributions.

The sheer size and longevity of the Roman world, however, has prevented this elitist view from triumphing completely. Poets, generals, and politicians were not the only ones to leave written records. Rome was a society of schools and letter writers, and literacy was widespread—although perhaps not uniformly—across the empire. Romans left records of both trivial and important aspects of their lives: most did not survive because they were written on perishable materials such as leather, clay, or papyrus (although papyrus did manage frequently to survive in the dry climate of Egypt). Messages that Romans scratched on walls have occasionally survived, and provide some of the oldest examples of graffiti.

1

The tombstone inscription is one of the most numerous and valuable types of written records to survive from Roman times. Many ancient civilizations produced funerary inscriptions; the impulse to leave some record of the deceased's life was characteristic of the Sumerians, Egyptians, Chinese, and many others. The Greeks commemorated their dead leaders and heroes with epitaphs in verse; a few of these verses have become as famous as the deeds and men they celebrate.

In the Hellenistic world, the tomb inscription, like the funeral oration, often took the form of an art self-consciously developed, and governed by the metric conventions of poetry. The tomb inscriptions of less exalted individuals were frequently shorter and not metered, but the majority of epitaphs that have survived from this era reflect the formality and even artificiality of Hellenism.

The earliest Roman tomb inscriptions reflect both an aesthetic and a view of death different from the Greek tradition.[1] The Roman who composed the matron's epitaph that begins this collection did not think he (or she) was creating literature, let alone poetry. The earliest Roman tomb inscriptions were often unmetered; they were viewed as only descriptive prose in an era which put little literary value on prose. To the modern reader, these inscriptions are of more than antiquarian or archeological interest. They can be considered "found poems," conveying considerable emotional power. Later prose tomb inscriptions also convey the feelings and sensibilities of the writers, but in a more deliberately rhetorical and self-conscious fashion. With the rise of Christianity in the third and fourth centuries, simpler and, in many respects, more "modern" sounding inscriptions appear, expressing very different sentiments about death and the afterlife.

---

[1] See J. M. C. Toynbee, *Death and burial in the Roman world.* Ithaca: Cornell University Press, 1971, 246-253

II
The Underworld

All the crowd ran headlong to the bank
Mothers and grown men, the lifeless bodies of
Great-hearted heroes, boys and unwed girls
And youths placed on their pyres in their parents' sight

As many as the leaves that fall deep in the wood
When Autumn's first cold blasts are felt
As many as the clouds of birds that rise
Above the ocean's face when the chill change
Of season drives them far across the sea
To seek out sunny lands,
So many stood beseeching to be allowed first
To cross the flood, raising their hands in longing
For the farther shore...[2]

Aeneid, VI, 305–314

Vergil's vision of Hades is still a familiar one: a shadow world populated
with shades of the departed, who squawk ineffectually instead of speaking, and who
endure an existence that seems a reduced or diluted version of their life on earth.
Hades is a place of gloom and chill, where the noble rub shoulders with the
depraved, and change and growth are permanently suspended. The renderings of
this place by Vergil, Ovid, and others are not empty literary commonplaces; they are
capable both of triggering emotional reactions in modern readers and of inspiring
writers such as Jean Cocteau or Samuel Beckett.[3] But did the Romans actually
believe that such a place existed? The answer to this question is complicated at the
onset when we remember that in Roman society numerous competing creeds jostled
one another in a basically tolerant coexistence. Along with the Italic pantheon of
Jupiter, Venus, Mercury, and other "official" gods, there flourished the Eleusinian
mystery cults, the worship of the god Mithras, the resuscitated Egyptian religions
that placed such great emphasis on the afterlife, and countless localized cults that
were cheerfully integrated into the greater Roman pantheon. Intellectuals unmoved
by the official cult of gods and deified emperors could choose from among Stoicism,

---

[2] All translations by the author.

[3] Jean Cocteau, "The testament of Orpheus," in *Two Screenplays: "The blood of a poet" and "The
testament of Orpheus*. Carol Martin-Speery, trans. Baltimore: Penguin, 1968, 69–144; Samuel Beckett,
"Imagination dead imagine" in *I can't go on, I'll go on: A selection from Samuel Beckett's work*.
Richard W. Seaver, ed. New York: Grove Press, 1976, 551–556.

which taught, in Marcus Aurelius's words, that death was only "one of the processes of nature"[4]; Epicureanism; or many other survivals of the Hellenistic philosophical schools. Or the cultured man or woman could opt for a thoroughgoing skepticism regarding all notions of an afterlife. At least one of the tomb inscriptions included here reflects this rejection of any hope of an existence after death. Reincarnation, a belief held by Pythagoreans, also had adherents. In the *Metamorphoses* of Ovid, a Pythagorean admonishes those who either believed in the old tales of the underworld or feared that death meant oblivion:

> O race so terrified by fear of chilly death!
> The spirit journeys here, then there,
> Making its home in whatever it desires.
>
> *Metamorphoses* XV, 153, 166–167

For the Christian, the afterlife is something entirely different.[5] The soul of the departed Christian

> Soared up to the abode
> Of the blessed
>
> *EG* 651

or

> Passed over without warning
> Into the heavenly kingdom.
>
> *RGM* 489

Such beliefs must have been comforting to parents who had lost a young child. These conceptions of heaven as a place for children contrast favorably with the grim picture of the shades of "boys and unwed girls" inhabiting Hades, or with the Stoic notion of the transformation of the soul into an incorporeal body that traveled though the heavens.[6]

---

[4] *Meditations*, IX, 3.

[5] See G. Sanders, "Afterlife: 3. In Greco-Roman Religion," *New Catholic Encyclopedia*. New York: McGraw-Hill, 1967, vol. 1, 188–192.

[6] Stoic philosophers disagreed about the nature of the afterlife. While Marcus Aurelius and Epictetus had little concern with the topic, Seneca proposed, in his letters and elsewhere, that the soul returned to the heavens whence it came to join the souls of the blessed. See Anna Lydia Motto, *Guide to the Thought of Lucius Annaeus Seneca.* Amsterdam: Adolf M. Hakkert, 1970, 61.

III
The Study of Tomb Inscriptions

With the decline of Roman institutions after the fifth century, the practice of erecting tombstones to the departed would appear to have waned. Yet the tombs of ancient Rome and their inscriptions never completely disappeared from sight during the Middle Ages. Some grave markers were incorporated into the structure of Christian churches, where they may be seen today. The medieval view of Rome, shaped by the fables of the *Gesta Romanorum* and by the gigantic ruins scattered across Europe, did not draw from tomb inscriptions for insight into the past.[7] Nor were these epitaphs recognized for their literary value. The return of interest in the Classical world that began in the fifteenth century, and the development of a more systematic approach to the study of the past, resulted in the cataloguing and drawing of architecture and tomb fragments bearing inscriptions. Typical of this work, which took place throughout the sixteenth and seventeenth centuries, is Broelmann's collection of inscriptions from Cologne (Colonia Agrippina), published in 1608.[8] Collections such as Broelmann's have helped modern historians deal with the significant numbers of inscriptions that have been lost or destroyed by war or urban expansion.

By the beginning of the nineteenth century, Roman archeology had advanced to the point where scholars in most of the larger cities of Europe had published collections of local antiquities. The rediscovery of Pompeii and Herculaneum, and their profusion of objects from everyday life, reminded scholars of the existence of hitherto ignored multitudes of people who made up the Roman Empire, while the exploration of crypts and catacombs in Rome itself brought to light details of life in Republican Rome and facts concerning the early Christian Church. In the Napoleonic era and afterward, governments and learned societies vied with one another to publish critical editions of classical works and to sponsor architectural and archeological studies. Adding to this atmosphere of increased interest in antiquity and international competition were improved communication and the involvement of prestigious national academies in the study of ancient history. The time was ripe for a comprehensive collection of all known inscriptions. In 1863, the Prussian Royal Academy of Sciences began to publish what was intended ultimately to be the definitive collection of Roman inscriptions, the *Corpus Inscriptionum Latinarum*. This mammoth project took decades to complete, and is still in the process of revision and emendation. Many of the Latin inscriptions I have translated in this book come from the *Corpus*.

---

[7] The *Gesta Romanorum* was a popular collection of entirely fictitious tales about Roman personalities, historical and imaginary. The *Gesta* formed an important source of information about Rome for medieval men and women, and was translated into several vernacular languages, including Middle English. See *Early English Versions of the Gesta Romanorum*. Sidney J.H. Herrtage, ed. London: Trubner and Co., 1879.

[8] S. Broelmann, *Epideigma, sive specimen historiae vet. omnis et purae florentis atque amplae civitatis Ubiorum ...* Köln: 1608.

The *Corpus* in its entirety contains thousands of inscriptions grouped geographically. Many inscriptions have survived only in the most fragmentary condition. The majority of more or less intact inscriptions are of little interest because they merely repeat stock phrases. Surviving Roman inscriptions often deal in a typically unoriginal way with the dedication of public buildings, aqueducts, and other structures, with boundaries and roads, and with the gods. Tomb inscriptions also make up a significant portion of the inscriptions collected in the *Corpus* and in other sources used, such as Kaibel's *Epigrammata Graeca*. An important work of analytical scholarship to which I owe a great deal is Richmond Lattimore's *Themes in Greek and Latin Epitaphs*. Not only did Lattimore identify a number of inscriptions of literary merit, but he contributed much toward categorizing both the themes and the literary commonplaces used in these inscriptions, as well as placing the inscriptions in proper theological and cultural contexts.

IV
This Selection

In culling out a small number of tomb inscriptions from the thousands of possible candidates, I have used the following criteria for selection. First, is the inscription or inscription fragment complete enough to communicate a sustained idea in translation? Second, is the inscription, beyond doubt, a grave inscription?

The two criteria involve the greatest amount of subjective judgment. In examining each sufficiently complete inscription, one must ask, Is this inscription original enough to have a place in a small anthology? The sentiment, "May the earth rest lightly on you," is new enough to the modern reader, but it was a cliché for the Romans, who used it repeatedly, either in its entire form or in an abbreviation. At the hands of a master such as Martial, the phrase regains all of its original power and more. Both the poem in which Martial reworks this idea and a more conventional "non-literary" epitaph are included to provide a sense of the accomplishment of Martial as well as the original source of his idea.

The second criterion is, does the epitaph have enough emotional power or aesthetic merit to allow it to be included in an anthology without being reworked excessively? One way around this highly subjective question is to opt for a series of translations "after" the grave inscriptions. Such an alternative is in many ways very attractive, as it gives the translator the freedom to "get inside" some of the obscure or hackneyed turns of phrase and create a vision of an entire world, complete with relationships between wives and husbands, masters and slaves, and children and parents. But to take the license of a Pound translating Chinese poetry or a Fitzgerald recreating the *Rubáiyát i*s risky when one is dealing with a collection of writings by several dozen authors. I chose instead to try to walk a middle ground with the anonymous inscriptions, taking some liberty to recast the unmetered prose, in which most of the inscriptions are written, into free verse that reflects, I hope, some of the understated pathos of the original.

With the handful of attributed literary epitaphs, the issues involved are quite different. It might be argued that epitaphs by Ovid or Martial come from a totally different genre and do not belong in such a collection as this. My response to this charge is there is no reason to claim that the literary epitaphs included here could not actually have existed as tomb inscriptions. The "Paris" celebrated by Martial was a famous actor, allegedly put to death by the emperor Domitian for a politically incorrect lampoon. The children commemorated in Martial's verses are said to have been the daughters of his slaves. The epitaphs included here, then, were no mere decorative literary effusions, but "functional" in the sense that they served the same purpose as those created as actual tomb inscriptions.

A fraction of the inscriptions in this anthology are in Greek, and come from the collection *Epigrammata Graeca*. Greek tomb inscriptions are common throughout Italy, and the evidence of the use of Greek by citizens other than the cosmopolitan upper classes is found in Gaul and elsewhere in the west. The inclusion of Greek epitaphs here reflects the character of the Roman world as a whole. Since the creation of epitaphs in Greek had a long and originally separate history, Greek epitaphs should not be regarded as always indistinguishable from Latin ones. Terminology may not always be interchangeable, a fact hidden here by the translation of both languages into English. In particular the Latin word *anima* and the Greek *psyche*, which are often both translated as "spirit" or "soul," take on different shades of meaning depending on whether the writer's perspective was pagan, orthodox Christian, or Gnostic.

For the Christian or Gnostic, *psyche* is used throughout the New Testament to signify the seat and center of life transcending the earthly changes and refines the understanding of this word. Greek also does not have a term which translates exactly the Latin word *pietas*, a key concept in Roman familial relations. In general, the Greek inscriptions come from a society that was blending Hellenistic and Roman values with, in some cases, an emerging Christian view of life and death, making them trickier to translate. My attempts here reflect a desire to show the degree to which these sometimes widely differing viewpoints shared the same emotional responses to the universal experience of bereavement.

The presence of early Christian tomb inscriptions in this collection adds another dimension to the task of presenting these translations as a coherent whole. The Christian epitaphs are contemporary with the inscriptions identified as "A Non-believer's Epitaph," "A Soldier's Grave," and a least a dozen others. Thus these epitaphs can be considered products of the same society, although they reflect a different world view.

The masterpieces of Martial also deserve inclusion here simply because they are so well crafted, so disciplined, and yet so refreshing in their directness. To exclude them from an anthology of Roman tomb inscriptions would be to ignore some of the finest examples of this genre, and to obscure the values that motivated ordinary people to compose these epitaphs. Starting from this position, I have taken one final liberty and included Catullus's famous "Hail and Farewell" to his brother, although it is not, strictly speaking, even a literary epitaph.

The presentation of the text is as follows: Wherever possible, a line drawing of the original inscription is given. It is followed by an edited version of the text, the translation, and notes.

V
Women and Children

He whom the gods love dies young

Plautus, *Bacchides*, 7:18

In the Roman world, as in all human societies that have existed before the arrival of modern hygiene and medicine, the mortality rate among young children and childbearing women was very high. Thus many surviving tomb inscriptions give clues as to how Roman society viewed women and children, and which traits were prized in each.

The married Roman woman was defined by her relationship to her husband, and her value was often determined by the fulfillment of certain expectations. An inscription from a freedwoman's tomb reads in part:

I was obedient to my elders
To my husband I was yielding

CIL 1194

A matron's fidelity and devotion were prized, largely for the honor that such conduct brought her husband. Martial closed a literary epitaph for a matron with a scarcely veiled reference to her sexual conduct:

What is more, my bedchamber
Received a rare honor, for only
One man was known
To my womanly modesty

Epigrams, 10.43

A wife was not her husband's equal partner, and she might be under the power of life and death held by the *pater familias* (head of the household) over all members of the family. Her actual duties were clear: she

cared for her home, spun wool, bore children and
raised them

CIL 1, 1007

And yet glimpses of more human relationships are discernible in many of the inscriptions written by bereaved husbands. While not legally an equal, a wife could grow to be a beloved companion and a valued friend. Inscriptions from the Christian era express the hope that husband and wife will be reunited in the hereafter. Yet even in the later centuries of the Principate, women remain in the

9

background of the Roman family. Even when we come upon an inscription that claims to be the words of the dead wife, we have the uneasy sense that the thoughts are not her own, but rather those of her husband.

Probably the epitaphs on children's graves were written by their parents. Although the legal and traditional status of children put them completely under the arbitrary power of the *pater familias*, children were valued and loved by their parents. Many gravestone inscriptions attest to the sincere and tender feelings adults held for their children. The loss of a child, although a commonplace event, could be a profound tragedy. But this tragedy was defined somewhat differently than it would be today. Boys were valued more highly than girls, in part because they were able to pass on the identity of the family throughout the *cognomen*. The greatest virtue of a Roman male offspring was *pietas*, best understood as a combination of filial devotion, dutiful conduct, and faithful performance of religious rituals. Aeneas, the determined hero of Vergil's *Aeneid*, represents the ultimate example of adult *pietas*, fulfilling his duty toward the gods, his country, and his family. Roman boys demonstrated *pietas* through complete obedience to the *pater familias* and by exhibiting the traditional Roman virtues of self-control, courage, and loyalty.

It is worth remembering that childhood and adolescence, in the sense that they are understood today, did not exist in the ancient world. The Roman children mourned by their parents were parts of a family unit rather than members of a special group. In particular, the girls were being prepared for a generally submissive role within the *familia* of their future husbands.

Yet even when we acknowledge the important differences between the Roman view of children and our own, there remains the persistent sense that bereaved Roman parents experienced the same emotions that all parents experience when their child dies. Not even the solace of the Christian view of the afterlife compensated for the feelings of loss and bewilderment that are discernible in so many of the inscriptions. While the differences between the classical views of the experience of loss intrigue the modern reader, it is the universal qualities conveyed in these tomb inscriptions that compel us to translate and read these records of these long departed people.

PLATE 1 (*RGM* 497)

Hic iacet Marti/nianus qui laeta / iuventae perdidiit / patribus lacrimas / dimisit. In aevo hic vix/it annos XXVI dies / XVI m(inus). In d(eo) ivit.

Date: Fourth to fifth century. *Laeta* should be taken here as a noun.

11

PLATE 2 (RGM 206)

C(aius) Vetieni(us) C(ai) f(ilius) / Pupinia Urbiqus / tubicem exs / legeoni I exs / testamento / f(aciendum) c(uravit).

Date: First half of the first century. Note the "illiterate" spelling *exs*.

TRANSLATOR'S NOTE

I have taken the liberty of giving titles to both the tomb inscriptions and the literary epitaphs. This is intended to clarify the theme of the inscription, and to set the mood that will help identity the particular quality of the epitaph that sets it apart from others. I have also changed the line lengths of many epitaphs. Roman and Greek inscription carvers were not too particular about how lines were divided, and often broke off lines and words as space required. I have tried to find line breaks that are true to the original sense of the inscription and that aid in viewing the epitaphs as poems. I have also followed the editorial practice of Richmond Lattimore, in his *Themes in Greek and Latin Epitaphs*, Urbana, Illinois: University of Illinois Press, 1962, and the editors of the *Corpus Inscriptionum Latinarum (CIL)* in restoring damaged, abbreviated, or incomplete inscriptions. Brackets ([ ]) in the original text indicate that letters or words have been supplied, and I have followed the usual custom of indicating untranslatable or grammatically incorrect passages with carets (< >).

ILLUSTRATIONS

All these plates are taken from the collection of the Römisch-Germanisches Museum in Cologne. While there are several important collections of Roman stone inscriptions elsewhere in Europe, this collection is significant because it contains examples from such a wide period of history (the first through seventh centuries C.E.) and because the inscriptions reflect the diversity and complexity of urban life under the Empire. Not all of the inscriptions portrayed in the plates may be considered literary in quality, but each sheds light on Roman society and its values.

ABBREVIATIONS USED IN CITATIONS

CE = *Carmina Latina Epigraphica.* Vols. 1–2, ed. Buecheler, Leipzig, 1895; vol. 3, ed. Lommatzsch, Leipzig, 1926.

CIL = *Corpus Inscriptionum Latinarum.* Berlin, 1862ff.

EG = Kaibel, G., *Epigrammata Graeca.* Berlin, 1878.

PA = Peck, H.T., and Arrowsmith, R., *Roman Life in Latin Prose and Verse.* New York, 1894.

RGM = *Wissenschaftliche Kataloge des Römisch-Germanischen Museums Köln.* Köln, 1975.

A ROMAN MATRON'S EPITAPH

Rome, near the bridge of St. Bartholomew

HOSPES·QVOD·DEICO·PAVLLVM·EST·ASTA·AC·PELLEGE
HEIC·EST·SEPVLCRVM·HAV·PVLCRVM·PVLCRAI·FEMINAE
NOMEN·PARENTES·NOMINARVNT·CLAVDIAM
SVOM·MAREITVM·CORDE·DEILEXIT·SOVO
5 GNATOS·DVOS·CREAVIT·HORVNC·ALTERVM
IN·TERRA·LINQVIT·ALIVM·SVB·TERRA·LOCAT
SERMONE·LEPIDO·TVM·AVTEM·INCESSV·COMMODO
DOMVM·SERVAVIT·LANAM·FECIT·DIXI·ABEI

HOSPES, QUOD DEICO PAULLUM EST; ASTA AC PELLEGE.
HEIC EST SEPULCRUM HAU PULCRUM PULCRAI FEMINAE.
NOMEN PARENTES NOMINARUNT CLAUDIAM.
SUOM MAREITUM CORDE DEILEXIT SOUO.
GNATOS DUOS CREAVIT, HORUNC ALTERUM   5
IN TERRA LINQUIT, ALIUM SUB TERRA LOCAT.
SERMONE LEPIDO, TUM AUTEM INCESSU COMMODO.
DOMUM SERVAVIT, LANAM FECIT. DIXI. ABEI.

CIL 1,1007

Stranger, what I have to say is brief,
So pause and read.
This rude tomb holds a fair woman's bones.
Named Claudia by her parents, she loved her husband in her heart
And bore two sons, one of whom yet lives.
Refined in speech, gentle in manner,
She cared for her home, spun wool.
Farewell.

Peck and Arrowsmith rendered the text in more regular Latin as follows:

Hospes, quod dico paullum est; asta ac perlege.
Hic est sepulcrum hau pulcrum pulcrae feminae:
Nomen parentes nominarunt Claudiam
Suum maritum corde dilexit suo.
Natos duos creavit: horum alterum   5
In terra linquit, alium sub terra locat.
Sermone lepido tum autem incessu commodo
Domum servavit, lanam fecit: dixi. Abi.

While this unmetered inscription, which dates probably from the second century
B.C. E., might be termed a "found poem," the seemingly self-conscious alliteration
in line 2 suggests that the author was striving for at least an ironic effect. The use of
abi as a valedictory is rare among grave inscriptions. A number of rare archaic
spellings are evident here, including *deico* for *dico*, *heic* for *hic*, *suom* for *suum*,
pulcrai for *pulcrae*, and *gnatos* (whose *g* was probably not silent) for *natos*.

TO HIS BROTHER

Asia Minor

MULTAS PER GENTES ET MULTA PER AEQUORA VECTUS
      ADVENIO HAS MISERAS, FRATER, AD INFERIAS,
UT TE POSTREMO DONAREM MUNERE MORTIS
      ET MUTAM NEQUIQUAM ALLOQUERER CINEREM,
QUANDOQUIDEM FORTUNA MIHI TETE ABSTULIT IPSUM,   5
      HEU MISER, INDIGNE FRATER, ADEMPTE MIHI.
NUNC TAMEN INTEREA HAEC, PRISCO QUAE MORE PARENTUM
      TRADITA SUNT TRISTI MUNERE AD INFERIAS,
ACCIPE FRATERNO MULTUM MANANTIA FLETU
      ATQUE IN PERPETUUM, FRATER, AVE ATQUE VALE.

Catullus 101

Many the nations and many the seas I traversed
To attend these sad funeral rites, my brother,
That I might honor you one last time
With an offering to the dead,
Speaking in vain to the silent ashes you have become,

Chance has taken you from me,
So prematurely carried off.
But now these offerings, in the custom of our fathers,
Are borne so sadly to your grave.
Receive them, bathed in your brother's tears,
And hear my greeting and farewell
Forever.

This famous poem has probably been translated as many times as any Latin verse. I have provided a particularly free translation of *mutam . . . cinerem* in line 4 both to clarify meaning and to give more weight to the final line of the first stanza of the translation. I have assumed that *fortuna* (line 5) does not refer specifically to the Goddess, and so have opted instead for a translation of "chance." I have not followed the usual custom of placing a translation of *ave atque vale* at the conclusion of the poem, translating *in perpetuum* instead as the last words.

PLATE 3 (RGM 222)

C(aius) Deccius L(uci) f(ilius) / Papiria Ticini / miles leg(ionis) XX / pequarius annor(um) / XXXV stipendioru(m) / XVI hic s(itus) est.

Date: First half of the first century.

PLATE 4 (*RGM* 196A)

D(is) M(anibus). C(aius) Iul(ius) Maternus / vet(eranus) ex leg(ione) I M(inervia) vi(v)us sibi / et Marie Marcellinae / coiiugi dulcissime / [et] castissisme obitae f(ecit).
Date: Second century.

21

SHE STOOD OUT

Rome (an exerpt)

HIC PERUSINA SITA EST, QUA NON PRETIOSIOR ULLA
FEMINA DE MULTIS, VIX UNA AUT ALTERA VISA;
SEDULA SERIOLA PARVA TAM MAGNA TENERIS.
'CRUDELIS FATI RECTOR DURAQUE PERSIPHONE,
QUID BONA DIRIPITIS EXUPERANTQUE MALA?'   5
QUAERITUR A CUNCTIS: IAM RESPONDERE FATIGOR;
DANT LACHRIMAS, ANIMI SIGNA BENIGNA SUI.
            FORTIS, SANCTA, TENAX, INSONS, FIDISSIMA CUSTOS,
MUNDA DOMI, SAT MUNDA FORAS, NOTISSIMA VOLGO,
SOLA ERAT, UT POSSET FACTIS OCCURRERE CUNCTIS;   10
EXIGUO SERMONE INREPREHENSA MANEBAT.
PRIMA TORO DELAPSA FUIT, CADEM ULTIMA LECTO
SE TULIT AD QUIETUM POSITIS EX ORDINE REBUS.
LANA CUI E MANIBUS NUNCQUAM SINE CAUSSA RECESSIT,
OPSEQUIOQUE PRIOR NULLA MORESQUE SALUBRES.   15
HAEC SIBI NON PLACUIT, NUMQUAM SIBI LIBERA VISA.
CANDIDA, LUMINIBUS PULCHRIS, AURATA CAPILLIS,
ET NITOR IN FACIE PERMANSIT EBURNEUS ILLAE,
QUALEM MORTALEM NULLAM HABUISSE FERUNT. . .

CE 1988

Here rests Perusina, who although she may not
Have seemed more precious or looked far different from other women,
Yet had great industry within her body's modest vessel.
"Cruel guide of Fate and harsh Persephone,
Why do you despoil the good while evils prevail?"
Everyone asks, and I am wearied with answering.
The gentle signs of her soul provoke our tears.

She was strong, inviolable, steadfast, blameless, a most faithful overseer.
Elegant at home, and elegant enough in public,
She stood out from the crowd.
She could manage all affairs; of few words,
She was above reproach.
She left the marriage bed first, and journeyed to her repose
With every household detail in order.
Wool never left her hands without due cause.
No one surpassed her in obedience
And sound conduct.
She did not seek to please herself, took no liberties,
Fair, with lovely eyes and golden hair,
Her face retained a pale beauty
Which (they say) no mortal had possessed. . .

A few Latin tomb inscriptions go far beyond formulae and indulge in lengthy
personal observations. This one speaks at least part of the time in the first person
and indicts Persephone, not often thought of as the *fati rector* (although an
alternative interpretation would make one of the *Parcae*, here unnamed, the villain).
The grammar and orthography are generally conventional; an exception is *seriola*
(l. 3), a rare diminutive of *seria*; also noteworthy are *exuperant* (*exsuperant*; l. 5) and
caussa (*causa*; l. 14). Along with the traditional virtues of the Roman matron,
Perusina possessed physical beauty, a point seldom stressed in classical tomb
inscriptions. The first few lines are somewhat obscure, and the present translation
preserves the ambiguity.

ARTEMIA

From Ancient Cologne

HIC IACIT ARTEMIA
DULCIS APTISSIMUS
INFANS ET VISU GRATA ET
VERBIS DULCISSIMA
CUNCTIS QUATTUOR   5
IN QUINTO AD XPM
DETULIT ANNOS
INNOCENS SUBI-
TO AD CAELESTI[A]
[REG]NA TRANSIVI[T]   10

RGM 489

Here lies Artemia,
A child bright and sweet,
Fair of visage, and most charming
In her speech.
Having lived four years,
In her fifth year she departed
To Christ, an innocent who
Passed over without warning
Into the heavenly kingdom.

l. 1: *Iacet* is the classical form; this orthography no doubt reflects local
pronunciation.

MARTINIANUS

From Ancient Cologne

HIC IACET MARTI-
NIANUS QUI LAETA
IUVENTAE PERDIDIIT
PATRIBUS LACRIMAS
DIMISIT. IN AEVO HIC VIX-   5
IT ANNOS XXVI DIES
XVI M[INUS]. IN D[EO] IVIT.

RGM 497

Here lies Martianus
Who lost the joys of youth
And left behind only tears
For his parents.
He lived 26 years, save 16 days.
He has gone to God.

PLATE 6 (RGM 495)

Leontius hic iacit fedelis / puer dulcissimus patri pientis/simus matri qui vixit annus / VII et mensis III et dies VI. In/ nocens funere raptus, / beatus mente, felix / et in pace reces/sit.

Date: Fifth to sixth century.

Note the nasalization of *pietissismus* into *pientissismus*.

LUPASSIUS

From Ancient Cologne

BLANDAM TE PIETAS
MORS INPIA FUNERE
TRISTI ABSTULIT ET
DULCIS RUPIT NOVA GAU-
DIA VITAE. NON LICUIT   5
CUPIDOS LONGUM
GAUDERE PARENTES. LUPASSIU[S]
PUER VIX[T] AN[NUM] I S[EMISSEM] III (MENSES).

RGM 496

Heartless death carried you off, tender child, with sad funeral rites
And robbed you of the early joys of sweet life.
Your fond parents were not allowed to delight in you
For long. Our boy Lupassius lived three years.

The last three inscriptions from Ancient Cologne to my knowledge have never been translated before into any modern language. All appear to date from the same era (late third to fifth centuries C.E.) and each seems to reflect a Christian perspective, which contains only occasional mention of the bliss of the afterlife. Syntactically, these inscriptions are less complex than many of the other inscriptions translated in this collection, and display a limited vocabulary. Nevertheless, they convey quite powerful emotions.

l. 1: *Blandam* is feminine in form, but may be a variant spelling of the masculine *blandum*.

NO ESCAPING THE GRAVE

Cremona

```
        M · sᵀAᵀIVS
         M·L· CHꞮLO
          HꞮC
       HEVS·Tv·VIAToR·LAS
  5   SE·QVi· ME · PRAETE
           REIS
       CVM · DIV · AMBVLA
       REIS ·TAMEN· HOC
       VENIVNDVM·EST·TIBI

  10  IN · F · P · X · IN · AG
          P·X
```

M. STATIUS M.L. CHILO HIC

HEUS TU VIATOR LASSE

QUI ME PRAETEREIS

CUM DIU AMBULAREIS, TAMEN HOC

VENIUNDUM EST TIBI.

CIL 1,2,2138

Marcus Statius Chilo, Freedman of Marcus,
Is here.
Ho, tired traveler
Who pass me by
You may walk
For a long time,
Yet here is where
You must come.

This inscription utilizes a formula (*heus viator...*) found on dozens of tombs. It is included here as a representative of this formula. The traditional formula is however varied in the last two lines. Note that although this inscription most probably dates from the late Republican period, freedman Marcus Statius Chilo or his family could afford a substantial tombstone.

l. 4 *ambulareis* = *ambulares, tamen hoc* = literally, "to this (place)"

A CHARIOTEER'S GRAVE

Tarraco, Italy

FACTIONIS VENETAE FUSCO SACRAVIMUS ARAM
DE NOSTRO CERTI STUDIOSI ET BENE AMANTES,
UT SCIRENT CUNCTI MONIMENTUM ET PIGNUS AMORIS.
INTEGRA FAMA TIBI, LAUDEM CURSUS MERUISTI.
CERTASTI MULTIS, NULLUM PAUPER TIMUISTI,   5
INVIDIAM PASSUS SEMPER FORTIS TACUISTI.
PULCHRE VIXISTI, FATO MORTALIS OBISTI.
QUISQUIS HOMO ES, QUAERES TALEM, SUBSISTE VIATOR,
PERLEGE. SI MEMOR ES, SI NOSTI QUIS FUERIT VIR
FORTUNAM METUANT OMNES DICES TAMEN UNUM: 10
FUSCUS HABET TITULOS MORTIS, HABET TUMULUM.
CONTEGIT OSSA LAPIS. BENE HABET. FORTUNA VALEBIS.
FUDIMUS INSONTI LACRIMAS. NUNC UNA: PRECAMUR
UT IACEAS PLACIDE. NEMO TUI SIMILIS.

CE 500

We the members of his team "Veneta,"
Dedicate this altar to Fuscus,
Our friend whom we eagerly
Supported and loved.
So that all might know
Of this monument and
Token of our love.
Unblemished fame was yours
You earned the praise of the race course
As you strove with many, fearing none,
Poor though you were.
And though suffering from others' jealousy

You always held your tongue like a man.
You lived beautifully:
As a mortal you met your fate.
Whoever you are, traveller, pause
And read this epitaph
To its end; and if you remember,
If you know what sort
Of man he was,
Seek such a man.
All, all fear fortune,
But you will add one thing:

Fuscus has his inscription, his tomb.
The stone covers his bones,
He is well.
You will prosper in good fortune.
We have poured out our tears for him who was without fault
But now one thing we pray:
That you may lie peacefully, Fuscus.
There was no one like you.

This lengthy inscription provides an unusually detailed look at the achievements of
the deceased and the sentiments that his companions in his *factio* felt for him.
Presumably these men were not part of literary society, and they appear to have
opted for a verse that possesses rhythmic rather than metric qualities. This
inscription then becomes a rare example of popular literary taste, where not only
may *tacuisti* be rhymed with *obisti*, but perhaps *vir* with *precamur* as well. An
alternative reading for *nunc una* is *nunc vina*; we may imagine his teammates
pouring libations over the charioteer's tomb.

I have chosen to translate *quaeres talem* (l. 8), since I take it to be the climax of the
inscription, several lines later in the English than where it appears in the Latin.

AN ANCIENT EXISTENTIALIST

Rome

QUID SUMUS AUT LOQUIMUR, VITA EST QUID DENIQ[UE NOSTRA?
VEL MODO NOBISCUM VIXIT HOMO, NUNC HOMO NO[N EST.]
STAT LAPIS ET NOMEN TANTUM, VESTIGIA NULLA.
QUID QUASI IAM VITA EST? NON EST QUOD QUAERERE CU[RES.]

CE 801

What are we
Or what do we say
At last this life is?
Just that a man has
Lived among us
And now is no more.
Just the stone
And the inscription remain,
And no other traces.
Now what
Is life?
It is nothing that
You should trouble yourself
To inquire about.

This is one of the most remarkable inscriptions to survive from the Roman period.
The use of *non est* in the sense of "no longer exists" is found in slightly different
forms among other tomb inscriptions, but the overwhelmingly skeptical tone of this
inscription is virtually without parallel. *Quasi* following an interrogative pronoun
(l. 4) is not common in classical Latin, but the inscription otherwise generally
conforms to classical usage. I have taken the liberty here, as elsewhere, to ignore the
line breaks in the Latin in order to call attention to the writer's unusual point of view.

PLATE 6 (RGM 247)

Romanus Atti f(ilius) Dar[danus] / eq(ues) al(ae) Afr(orum) tur(ma) Firmani an(norum) XXX st[ip(endiorum)---]./H(eres) t(estamento) f(aciendum) c(uravit).

Date: First century C.E. The *RGM* catalogue contains photographs that show that this fragment is part of a larger stone which, surprisingly, has also survived. This fragment is included to illustrate the condition in which many inscriptions are when found.

33

PULVIS ET UMBRA

Rome

SEI·QVIS·HAVET·NOSTRO · CONFERRE · DOLORE
ADSIT·NEC·PARVEIS·FLEREQVE·AD·LACHRYMIS
QVAM·COLVIT·DVLCI · GAVISVS · AMORE · PVELLA
IN FELIX·VNICA·QVEI·FVERAT
FATORVM · TEMPORA · NVMPHE
A · DOMV·CARA·SVEIS·TEGITVR
VS · ET · EO · LAVDATA · FIGVRA
C·EST·PARVOS·ET·OSSA·CINIS

5

SEI QUIS HAVET NOSTRO CONFERRE DOLORE [M],

ADSIT NEC PARVEIS FLERE QUEAD LACHRYMIS

QUAM COLUIT DULCI GAVISUS AMORE PUELLA [M]

[HIC LOCAT] INFELIX UNICA QUEI FUERAT,

[DUM CONTRACTA] SINUNT FATORUM TEMPORA NUMPHE,   5

[NUNC EREPT]A DOMU CARA SUEIS TEGITUR.

[OMNE DECUS VOLT]US ET EO LAUDATA FIGURA

[UMBRA LEVIS NUN]C EST ET PARVOS ET OSSA CINIS.

CIL 1,2,1222

If any have a sorrow to compare to ours
Let him draw near and weep freely.
Here a grieving parent laid to rest
Nymphe, his only daughter, whom he
Cherished with a gentle love while yet he could,
In what little time the Fates allowed.

Now she who was so dear to her family
Has been carried off from her home and is covered by earth.
Her fair face and figure praised as fair
Now are an insubstantial shadow,
Her bones but a bit of ash.

34

The restorations of the text were provided in *CIL* which notes "*numphe aut nomen proprium aut pro nova nupta.*"

This inscription poses many grammatical problems. The restoration of [*hic locat*] (l. 4) introduces a verb that normally takes a direct object. If the line is translated literally with this addition, then *puella. . .infelix unica* must be the subject. But what is the unhappy girl placing? I have chosen to take *infelix* as masculine, agreeing with *gavisus*, and make *puella . . . unica* the direct object of *locat*. Might the beginning of l. 4 be better rendered as *hic est*?

l. 1 *havet* = *habet*. This is a relatively unusual variation, not readily identified with any known Italic dialect.

l. 4 *quei* = *qui* (or possibly *cui* or *quae*)

l. 6 *sueis* = *suis*

A MAN OF LETTERS

Algeria

```
        D    M    S
HISCE  LOCIS  FLORI  REQVIESCV
NT  OSSA  SEPVLTA  ⌀ AETATS
PRIME  MISERNDO  FVNE
RE  RAPTO  DITS  AD  NFER
NAS  SEDES  LVCOSQVE  ÞORVM
QVEM  DOCTA  STVDIS  ORNARAT
DIVA  THALIA  QVI  PROPE  VI
CENOS  BS  IAM  SVPLEVERAT
NNOS  N  LACHESIS  BREVIA  RVPIS
SE  STAMNA  FVSO⌀PRO  DOLOR  VI
NVLL  DECREA  RVMERE  FAS  EST
PARCARVM  DIVA  DVROSQVE  EVA
DERE  CASVS  ⌀ H  S  E
```

D(IS) M(ANIBUS) S(ACRUM).
HISCE LOCIS FLORI REQUIESCUNT OSSA SEPULTA
AETATIS PRIMAE MISERANDO FUNERE RAPT[I]
DITIS AD INFERNAS SEDES LUCOSQUE PIORUM.
QUEM DOCTA STUDIIS ORNARAT DIVA THALIA,   5
QUI PROPE VICENOS BIS IAM SUPLEVERAT ANNOS,
NI LACHESIS BREVIA RUPISSET STAMINA FUSO.
PRO DOLOR VI NULLI DECRETA RUMPERE FAS EST
PARCARUM DIVA DUROSQUE EVADERE CASUS.
H(IC) S(ITUS) E(ST).   10

Sacred to the shades of the departed
The bones of Florus lie buried in this place.
Florus, who was carried off in youth with
Sad funeral rites
To shadowed home of Pluto
and the graves of the virtuous.

The learned muse, Thalia
Graced him with talents.
He had completed
Almost two score years on earth
When Lachesis cut short
His brief thread of life
On her spindle.

O sorrow!
No force on earth
Can abridge the divine decrees
Of the fates
Or escape
What must befall.

Here he is buried.

CIL 8,8870

The text of this inscription is intact and poses no particular problems with regard to vocabulary or syntax. Of special note is the implication that although Florus was almost forty years old, hardly young by Roman standards, his death was regarded as untimely. The *fusus* was a customary attribute of the Fates, and is mentioned by Vergil and Ovid. The final line, *Parcarum . . . casus*, filled with harsh *c*s and *s*s and long vowels, seemed to call for a somber, even stark, ending. The last three lines of the translation, although their line breaks bear no resemblance to the original, are an attempt to provide this.

AN ACTOR'S GRAVE

Near Rome

QUISQUIS FLAMINIAM TERIS, VIATOR,
NOLI NOBILE PRAETERIRE MARMOR.
URBIS DELICIAE SALESQUE NILI,

ARS ET GRATIA, LUSUS ET VOLUPTAS,
ROMANI DECUS ET DOLOR THEATRI   5
ATQUE OMNES VENERES CUPIDINESQUE
HOC SUNT CONDITA, QUO PARIS, SEPULCRO.

Martial 11.13

Whoever you are, traveller,
Trudging along the Via Flaminia,
Do not overlook this
Monument of noble marble.
The delight of Rome,
The wit of Egypt,
Artistry and grace,
The ornament and now the sorrow
Of the Roman theatre
And all the loves and cupids
Are buried there.
Which is to say
This is the tomb of
Paris.

This poem posed the special problem of conveying some of the terse diction of Martial while preserving the richness of his evocative vocabulary. I did not keep the division between the two Latin stanzas, since in my translation the second stanza would have been so long as to upset the unity of the poem. In the end it seemed impossible to render the poem in anything close to its set of line breaks; hence this is a particularly free translation. Ending the poem with the final line "Paris" is an attempt to reflect the finality and isolation of the lone word *sepulcro*.

PLATE 7 (RGM 252)

T(itus) Flavius Bassus Mucalae / f(ilius) Dansala eq(ues) alae Nori/coru(m) tur(ma) Fabi Pudentis /
an(norum) XXXXVI stip(endiorom) XXVI. H(eres) f(aciendum) c(uravit).
Date: First century A.D.

ON THE DEATH OF A LITTLE GIRL

HANC TIBI, FRONTO PATER, GENETRIX FLACCILLA, PUELLAM
    OSCULA COMMENDO DELICIASQUE MEAS,
PARVULA NE NIGRAS HORRESCAT EROTION UMBRAS
    ORAQUE TARTAREI PRODIGIOSA CANIS.
IMPLETURA FUIT SEXTAE MODO FRIGORA BRUMAE,   5
    VIXISSET TOTIDEM NI MINUS ILLA DIES.
INTER TAM VETERES LUDAT LASCIVA PATRONOS
    ET NOMEN BLAESO GARRIAT ORE MEUM.
MOLLIA NON RIGIDUS CAESPES TEGAT OSSA, NEC ILLI,   10
    TERRA, GRAVIS FUERIS: NON FUIT ILLA TIBI.

Martial 5.34

My parents Fronto and Flaccilla, I commend to you
    This girl, my pet and my delight,
That Hell's shadows and the beast that guards its gate
    May not frighten Erotion.
She would have been just six years old
    Had she lived but six days more.
May she play among her elders with a light heart
    And in a childish voice call out my name.
O loam, press gently on her tender bones, nor earth,
    shall you have rested heavily on her,
    For gently she trod on you.

Tradition maintains that this child was the daughter of one of Martial's slaves, who is on the way to join Martial's parents (and thus her grandparents?) in the underworld. In the translation of *Tartarei* (l. 4) I have chosen "Hell's" over the more accurate "Hades'" for the more vivid and terrible image that the former term summons up. Martial used the convention of "rest lightly" in an evocative fashion here. Since the same sentiment is expressed several other times in this anthology, the challenge was to retain both the freshness the phrase conveys to the first-time reader as well as the skill with which Martial recast this stock phrase.

41

THE POET OVID'S EPITAPH: WRITTEN BY HIMSELF

Tomis

HIC EGO QUI IACEO TENERORUM LUSOR AMORUM
    INGENIO PERII NASO POETA MEO
AT TIBI QUI TRANSIS NE SIT GRAVE QUISQUIS AMASTI
    DICERE NASONIS MOLLITER OSSA CUBENT

Tristia III, 3, 73–76

I who lie here was a writer
Of tales of tender love,
Naso the poet, done in by my
Own ingenuity
You who pass by, should you be
A lover, may you
Trouble yourself to say that
Naso's bones
May rest softly.

It is supposed that the *Tristia* were written in the Black Sea settlement of Tomis, where the poet was banished after his "carmen et error." The verses here have more than a hint of self-pity, and suggest that the *lusor amorum* may have not only played with tales of love, but outsmarted himself as well. Ovid has drawn upon some of the stock phrases of tomb inscriptions: *qui transis* echoes the notion of the call to the passing traveler, while *molliter ossa cubent* is a variation on "may the earth rest lightly." It was possible to translate these lines almost entirely literally; I have only made *amasti* a noun phrase and given it more of the force of the present tense.

PLATE 8 (*RGM* 146)

Deae / Vagdavercusti / Titus Flavius / Constans praef(ectus) / praet(orio) em(inentissimus) v(ir).
Date: c. 164. This inscription, the only one in this collection that is not strictly speaking a tomb inscription, appears on an altar.

43

A PEACEABLE MAN

Ager Tusculanus, Italy

TE ROGO, PRAETERIENS FAC MORA ET PERLEGE VERSUS
QUOS EGO DICTAVI ET IUSSI SCRIBERE QUENDAM.
EST MIHI TERRA LEVIS MERITO, SED QUIESCO MARMORE CLAUSUS
REDDEDI DEPOSITUM, COAGLAVI SEMPER AMICOS,
NULLIUS THALAMOS TURBAVI, NEMO QUERETUR.   5
CONIUNX KARA MIHI MECUM BENE VIXIT SEMPER HONESTE.
PRAESTITI QUOD POTUI, SEMPER SINE LITE RECESSI.
UNUS AMICUS ERAT TANTUM MIHI QUI PRAESTITIT OMNIA SEMPER
HONESTE,
       T. FL. HERMES V(IATOR) Q(UAESTORIUS).
TUNC MEUS ADSIDUE SEMPER BENE LUXIT, AMICE, FOCUS.

CE 477

I ask you as you pass by
Take a moment's pause and read
The lines I've dictated and
Ordered to be written.
The earth rests lightly on me
Which is as it should be.
And I lie quietly, encased in marble.
I've repaid my debt.

I always had a cluster of friends.
I disturbed no one's bedchamber, and
No complaint was lodged against me.
My dear wife lived with me
In harmony and always virtuously.

I performed the tasks I could,
Always gave place without recourse to the law.
I had just one friend who did all things honorably.
He surpassed all others in virtue:
Titus Flavius Hermes, a court officer of quaestorian
       rank.
In those days my hearth always burned brightly, friend.

The actual voice of this inscription is a little unclear. The first seven lines are filled with praise for the deceased, but in l. 8 a nameless friend is also lauded; presumably he paid to have the tombstone erected. The very unusual spelling of *kara* (*cara*) in l. 6 points to the relatively unlettered background of the stonecutter or the composer of the inscriptions. Other points of interest include a reference to the faithfulness of the deceased, a switch from the usual emphasis placed on a wife's fidelity, and the rather un-Roman phrase *semper sine lite recessi* (l. 7). The name Titus Flavius suggests a date after the middle of the first century.

A FAMILY MAN

Spoleto, Italy

QUAMVIS SAEVA TUOS PROPERANS MORS RUPERIT ANNOS
    NEC RATA SINT VITAE TEMPORA LONGA TUAE,
SINT TIBI PRO RAPIDO TAMEN HAEC SOLACIA LETO,
    QUOD CLARA GENERIS NOBILITATE VALES,
FLORET CELSA DOMUS, SUBOLES CLARIQUE NEPOTES,   5
    NON EST IN CASU MORS METUENDA TIBI,
NEC TE SOLLICITAT SAEVISSIMA CURA MINORUM,
    ET SERVAT CASTOS UXOR AMATA TOROS
LINQUENS TE PROPTER, IOHANNES, GAUDIA VITAE,
    [SIQUE DEO PLACEAT,] IAM CARITURA DIE.

CE 1849

Although fierce rushing death cut short your years
Nor could the years of your life (had it been long)
    be reckoned,
Still let there be these comforts in your sudden death:
You endure in the famous nobility of your line
Your lofty house flourishes, distinguished are your children
    and grandchildren.
Nothing in the happenstance of death should cause you fear;
You are not cruelly troubled by the care of your offspring.
Your beloved wife keeps chaste your marriage bed and
For your sake leaves behind the joys of life, John,
And if it please God, will soon depart from the light of this day.

l. 2: My parenthetical interpretation of *vitae tempora longa* is an attempt to reconcile the phrase with *pro rapido . . . leto*. l. 4. *Generis* most probably refers to the wider clan, although Vergil, among others, used it to refer specifically to direct descendants.

l. 6: An elegant line expressing a sentiment common throughout pagan and Christian society.

l. 9: *Iohannes*: The deceased's name points strongly, if not decisively, to a Christian origin for this inscription.

l. 10: This emendation provided by *CE* echoes an often-repeated phrase, and is therefore very probable.

ONLY ASLEEP

Syria, 2nd Century C.E.

Ὕπνος ἔχει σε, μάκαρ, πολυήρατε δῖε Σαβῖνε,
    καὶ ζῆς ὡς ἥρως καὶ νέκυς οὐκ ἐγένου·
εὕδεις δ' ὡς ἔτι ζῶν ὑπὸ δένδρεσι σοῖς ἐνὶ τύμβοις·
    ψυχαὶ γὰρ ζῶσιν τῶν ἄγαν εὐσεβέων.

EG 433

Sleep holds you fast
Blessed and beloved, noble Sabinus.
And you live on as a hero.
You have not become a corpse.
You sleep well as if alive.
Under the trees amidst the tombs of your ancestors,
For the souls of the truly pious
Go on living.

This graceful little verse contains no stereotyped phrases and, while revealing little of the character of the deceased, conveys a belief in immortality that seems sincerely held. The meaning of σοῖς is a little uncertain; I have chosen to translate it as modifying τύμβοις. Otherwise, the meaning of the verse is clear.

PLATE 9 (*RGM* 196B)

D(is) Liberalinio M(anibus) / Probino tribuno / Q praetoriano et / Liberaliniae Q Pro/ binae filiae eiius. Bar/barinia Accepta m/arito et filiae obitis.

Date: Second half of the third century.

ON A SOLDIER'S TOMB

Asia Minor

T · CISSONIVS · Q · F · SER · VE*t*
LEG · V̄ · GALL · DVM · VIXI
*bi*BI · LIBENTER · BIBI*te* · VOS
QVI · VIVITIS
5   P · C*is*SONIVS · Q · *f* · SER·FRATER
F*ec*I T

T. CISSONIUS Q.F. SER. VET. LEG. V. GALL.
DUM VIXI, BIBI LIBENTER: BIBITE VOS QUI VIVITIS.

CIL 3,293

I was Titus Cissonius brother of Quintus(?) veteran of the fifth Gallic
    Legion.
While I lived I drank freely.
You who still live, drink!

This tombstone, described in *CIL* as embedded in the wall of a mosque in Turkey,
was erected by the brother of the deceased. The meaning of *Q.F.* is most likely
Quinti frater. The date of the inscription cannot easily be placed, although the
increased number of legions stationed in Asia Minor after the middle of the third
century may point to this period.

PLATE 10 (*RGM 354*)

Aquilo C(ai) et M(arci) Versulati/um l(ibertus) / h(ic) s(itus) e(st). P(atroni) f(aciendum) c(uraverunt) / et Murano l(iberto).

Date: First half of the first century. A *libertus* was a freedman.

BEFORE HIS TIME

Spain

D ⊘ M ⊘ S ⊘
M · CALP · LVCIVS
DECVRIO
FLERE · CVPIS · QVICVMQVE · MEOS
5 IN MARMORE CASVS · SISTE · PARV
LACRIMAS SORTE MISERANDVS · INIQVA
sic AMISSISSE PIVM PAI I I DEDITQ_ · SEPVL
CRO QVAM PENE IA ⩶ ESSE · ANN · XXVI
M · VI · D · QVE · VIII · CONDITVS EGO IACEO
10 MISERO GENITORE RELICTO IAM MA
TER MISERA PALMISQVE VBERA TV
NDENS ET SOROR INFELIX COMI
TANTVR LVCTIBVS AMBE CONIVX
CARA MEA RELICTA CVM PARVO
15 LO FILIO CASTA MATER VIDVA
NO MIHI VITA SVPESTAT ⊘
QVI NOSTRVM TVMVLVM ONO
RAVIT CORPVS FOSAIMAQIIETS
PIHI PARENTES REGNAQVE · MVN
20 DI TENETES HIC EGO SEPVLTVS
IACEO PLACIDVSQVE QVIESCO
H ⊘ S ⊘ S ⊘ T ⬦ T ⬦ L

FLERE CUPIS QUICUMQUE MEOS IN MARMORE CASUS,
SISTE PARU(M) LACRIMAS SORTE(M) MISERANDUS INIQUA(M),
AMISISSE PIUM PATRE, DEDITQ(UE) SEPULCRO,
QUAM PENE IAM . . . ESSE
     ANN(OS) XXVI M(ENSES) VI D(IES)QUE VIII   5
CONDITUS EGO IACEO MISERO GENITORE RELICTO.
IAM MATER MISERA PALMISQUE UBERA TUNDENS
ET SOROR INFELIX COMITANTUR LUCTIBUS AMB(A)E.
CONIUX CARA MEA RELICTA CUM PARVOLO FILIO

CASTA MATER VIDUA; NO(N) MIHI VITA SUPE(R)STAT   10
QUI NOSTRUM TUMULUM ONORAVIT CORPUS EOSAIMA QUIETE
PIHI PARENTES REGNA QUI MUNDI TENETIS,
HIC EGO SEPULTUS IACEO PLACIDUSQUE QUIESCO.

CIL 2,1088

Whoever you are who wish
To lament my descent into the tomb,
Pause a bit and take pity on my unkind fate. . .

I completed twenty six years,
Six months and
Eight days.
I lie here buried having left
My poor father.
Now my poor mother beats
Her breasts with her hands
And my unhappy sister joins her.

My precious wife remains
With our little son; a chaste mother
And now a widow.
Nothing of my life
Endures.
Who decorates my tomb
And [lets] my body [rest]?

Goodly parents, who cling yet
To this world,

Here I lie buried and
Peacefully I rest.

This inscription, which was apparently found in poor condition, is of note because of
its highly individual and personal references. Some nonstandard spellings include
comintantur for *comitantur* (l. 8), *parbolo* for *parvulo* (l. 9), and *onoravit* for
honoravit (l. 10). Only those portions of the inscription that seemed coherent are
translated here. Despite these difficulties, the inscription retains considerable power,
both in its vivid portrayals of a mourning family, and in the grace of the last two
lines, where the image of mortals clinging to earth is contrasted with the peace of
death.

PLATE 11 (RGM 245)

L(ucius) Crispi f(ilius) cives / Marsacus eq(ues) alae / Affro(rum) turma Flavi / ann(orum) XXVIII stip(endiorum) VIIII. / H(eres) f(aciendum) c(uravit).

Date: Second half of the first century. A number of African legions were stationed in Cologne until at least the third century.

54

PARTING

LAGGE FILI BENE QUIESCAS
MATER TUA ROGAT TE
UT ME AD TE RECIPIAS
VALE!

PA 19

Quiet now, Laggus, my son,
Your mother asks you
That you take me to you
Farewell.

Peck and Arrowsmith provide this inscription without any further citation, and I have been unable to locate an earlier citation for this inscription. If the mother's voice is heard here, it is a relatively rare instance of maternal sentiments conveyed on a tombstone. The name Laggus may point to a Germanic origin of this inscription.

THE GARMENT OF THE SOUL

Near Naples

Αἰλιανῶι τόδε [σῆμα] πατὴρ ἀγαθῶι πι[νυτῶι τε,
    θ[νη]τὸν κηδ[εύσα]ς σῶμα· τὸ δ᾽ ἀθάνατ[ον
ἐς μακά[ρ]ων ἀνόρο[υσ]ε κέαρ· ψυχὴ γὰρ ἀείζ[ως,
    ἢ τὸ ζῆν παρέχει [κ]αὶ θεόφιν κατέβη.
ἴσχεο [σὺ] στοναχῶν, πά[τε]ρ, ἴσχε δέ, μῆτερ, ἀδελφούς·   5
    σῶ[μα] χ[ι]τὼν ψυχῆς· τ[ὸ]ν δὲ θεὸν σέβε μου.

EG 651

His father built this tomb for Aelianus, the good and wise,
Out of concern
For his son's mortal body.
But the immortal heart
Soared up to the abode
Of the blessed
For everliving is the soul
That offers life and
Comes down from God.

Though you mourn,
Restrain yourself, my father:
Mother, restrain my brothers.

The body is but the garment
Of the soul.
Reverence that part of me
Which is God's.

As reported in *CIL*, this inscription from central Italy was in poor condition and portions were only minimally legible. κέαρ· (l. 3) is generally translated as "heart" although the implication here extends to something very close to the ψυχῆς [spirit] referred to in l. 6. The χ[ι]τὼν in l. 6 was the common garment of both men and women. τ[ὸ]ν δὲ θεὸν σέβε μου in the same line poses a special challenge in translation; literally, it means "reverence my god." The theology expressed here prompted Kaibel to speculate, *"Defunctus fortasse Pythagoreus fuit."*

A VICTIM OF FEVER

AEOLIDOS CANACE IACET HOC TUMULATA SEPULCHRO,
    ULTIMA CUI PARVA SEPTIMA VENIT HIEMPS.
A SCELUS, A FACINUS! PROPERAS QUI FLERE, VIATOR,
    NON LICET HIC VITAE DE BREVITATE QUERI:
TRISTIUS EST LETO LETI GENUS: HORRIDA VULTUS   5
    APSTULIT ET TENERO SEDIT IN ORE LUES,
IPSAQUE CRUDELES EDERUNT OSCULA MORBI
    NEC DATA SUNT NIGRIS TOTA LABELLA ROGIS.
SI TAM PRAECIPITI FUERANT VENTURA VOLATU,
    DEBUERANT ALIA FATA VENIRE VIA.   10
SED MORS VOCIS ITER PROPERAVIT CLUDERE BLANDAE,
    NE POSSET DURAS FLECTERE LINGUA DEAS.

Martial 11, 91

Canace, a little child of Aeolis, lies entombed here,
Whose seventh winter was her last.
O crime! O wickedness! You who hasten to weep, O traveler,
Lament not here the shortness of life.
Sadder than death itself is the form it takes:
A fearful infection ravaged her face and
Settled on her tender mouth. Her very kisses
Were devoured by cruel illnesses, nor were her
Lips given to the black funeral pyre
In their normal state.
If the fates were going to come
In such a rapid flight
They should have come another way!
But death hastened to close the passage of
Her pleasant voice, lest her tongue
Dissuade the harsh goddesses.

Like virtually all of Martial's epigrams, this one survives in uncorrupted form in a manuscript. Canace was probably the child of one of Martial's slaves, with whom he apparently maintained cordial relations. The child's name and that of her parent (father?) may point to a Greek origin. While we may assume that this epigram was composed with a larger reading public in mind, the verse is free of artificiality and contrivance. As is the case with other epigrams of Martial, it is not known whether this verse was ever actually used as a tomb inscription. Of special note is the term *lues* in l. 6. In classical times, this word could refer to any plague, pestilence, or disfiguring disease; much later in the Renaissance, it was specifically employed to refer to syphilis.

A TOMB OF TWO YOUNG BOYS

Found in the church of St. Ursula, Cologne

HOC HOC SEPVLCRVM RESPICE
QVI CARMEN ET MVSAS·AMAS
ET NOSTRA COMMVNI LEGE
LACRIMANDA TITVLO NOMINA
5 NAM NOBIS PVERIS SIMVL
ARS VARIA PAR·AETAS ERAT
EGO CONSONANTI · FISTVLA
SIDONIVS ACRIS PERSTREPENS
HOC CARMEN HAEC ARA HᴵC CNIS
10 PVERI SEPVLCRVM EST XANTIAE
QVI MORTE ΛCERBA RAPTVS EST
IAM DOCTVS IN COMPENDIA
TOT LITERARVM Ɔ NOMNVM
NOTARE CVRRENTI STILO
15 QVOD LINGVA CVRRENS DICERET
IAM NEMO SVPERARET LEGEN/
IAM VOCE ERILI COEPERAT
AD OMNE DICTATVM VOLANS
AVREM VOCARI ΦT PROXIMAM
20 HEV MORTE PROPERA CONCIDIT
ARCANA QVI SOLVS SVI
SCITVRVS DOMINI FVIT

HOC HOC SEPULCRUM RESPICE
QUI CARMEN ET MUSAS AMAS
ET NOSTRA COMMUNI LEGE
LACRIMANDA TITULO NOMINA.
NAM NOBIS PUERIS SIMUL   5
ARS VARIA, PAR AETAS ERAT.
EGO CONSONANTI FISTULA
SIDONIUS ACRIS PERSTREPENS.
HOC CARMEN, HAEC ARA, HIC CINIS

60

PUERI SEPULCRUM EST XANTIAE,   10
QUI MORTE ACERBA RAPTUS EST.
IAM DOCTUS IN COMPENDIA
TOT LITERARUM ET NOMINUM
NOTARE CURRENTI STILO
QUOD LINGUA CURRENS DICERET.   15
IAM NEMO SUPERARET LEGENS
IAM VOCE ERILI COEPERAT
AD OMNE DICTATUM VOLANS
AUREM VOCARI AT PROXIMAM.
HEU MORTE PROPERA CONCIDIT   20
ARCANA QUI SOLUS SUI
SCITURUS DOMINI FUIT

CIL 13,8355

You who love song and the Muses
Look upon this tomb, and read
Our names, which should provoke tears
As they are written here together as they are.
For we were boys of the same age
But with different gifts.
I, Sidonius, with my harmonious pipe
Was keen to fill the air with music.
This verse, this altar, these ashes
Are the tomb of the youth Xantia
Whom harsh death carried off.
He was already skilled in writing with his running stylus
In a catalog of so many
Letters and names
All that a fluent tongue could utter,
Already no one surpassed him in reading
He came flying at his master's call
And he had already begun to be called by his
Master, "the ear nearest his own."

Alas, swift death struck down
The one who alone was about
To learn his own
Master's arts.

l. 1: The reason for the second *hoc* is not clear.

ll. 16–23: The meaning here, in what has been so far a fairly straightforward inscription, is unclear. *Erili* can refer to either the head of a family or the master of a household. Could it be a reference to a deity, or even the Christian God? If so, then the meaning might be that the youth is being summoned to hear a more important divine message than the ones he has been writing down. The rest of the inscription, however, would seem to argue against this interpretation. The appearance of the subjunctive *superaret* may imply a contrary to fact situation ("would have surpassed"), or may simply be evidence of how the subjunctive and indicative were already starting to fuse in common usage. ll. 20–22 are easier to understand: here *dominus* clearly refers to an earthly master.

PLATE 12 (*RGM 494*)

In oh tumolo / reqiescet / in pace bone / memorie / Leo. Vixet an/nus XXXXXII. Tr/ansiet no/no Id(u)s Ohtub/eres.

Date: Sixth or seventh century C.E.

This inscription is a fascinating example of very late Latin, in which intitial *h* has been dropped, and *cs* are apparently being replaced by either a rough breathing or some similar vocalization. The question remains: was this very late form of Latin the spoken language in the Rheinland as late as the sixth century?

63

WHEN A CHILD DIES

North Africa

GAVDIA QVE DEDERAT RAPVIT FORTVNA REPENTE
/ / / / / / Es LVCTVS CONVERTIT VOTA PARENTVM
NAM PVER HOC PARVVS VITAEQ E LIMINE RAPTVS
GINGA SITVS TVMVLO EST INDIGNI VVLNERA PATRIS
5   A DOLOR ET GEMITVS INLVSAQ VOTA TVORVM
NON TAMEN AD MANES SED CAELI AD SIDERA PERGIS

GAUDIA QUE DEDERAT RAPUIT FORTUNA REPENTE
[INQ(UE) ACR]ES LUCTUS CONVERTIT VOTA PARENTUM;
NAM PUER HOC PARVUS VITAEQ(UE) E LIMINE RAPTUS
GINGA SITUS TUMULO EST, INDIGNI VULNERA PATRIS.
A! DOLOR ET GEMITUS INLUSAQ(UE) VOTA TUORUM!   5
NON TAMEN AD MANES, SED CAELI AD SIDERA PERGIS.

CIL 8,8567

Fortune, which has bestowed happiness
Upon his parents, swiftly turned their
Hopes into sharp cries of lamentation.

For their little boy was carried off
From the very threshold of life.
Ginga lies in this tomb
A wound to his father
Who did not deserve such a blow.

Ah, sorrow and mourning and
Your parents' hopes reduced
To a mockery!
But not to the shades of the departed but
Rather to the stars of heaven
You are journeying.

Here we see the use of an acrostic to form the name "Ginga" in the first vertical line of the inscription. The origin of this tomb has been variously identified as Safi, in modern day Morocco, very near the southernmost edge of Roman territory, and Setif, in Algeria, with the latter location the more probable. The name of the boy is presumably North African. The meter is dactylic hexameter, and the syntax and orthography conform to classical usage. This inscription is one of the best examples of a self-conscious attempt to create a literary memorial. The reference to the deceased (not merely Ginga's soul) ascending to the stars does not necessarily imply belief in Christianity; as far back as the Orion myth, pagan mortals were envisioned as ascending into the sky.

The use of *repente* (l. 1) suggests Ginga may have been very young, making the creation of this ambitious inscription all the more unusual.

LIVE FOR TODAY

Rome

P R I M A E
P O M P E I A E
O S S V A · H E I C
FORTVNA · SPONDET · MVLTA
5   MVLTIS · PRAESTAT · NEMINI · VIVE IN DIES
ET · HORAS · NAM · PROPRIVM · EST · NIHIL
SALVIVS · ET · HEROS · DANT

PRIMAE POMPEIAE OSSUA HEIC.
FORTUNA SPONDET ·MULTA· MULTIS, PRAESTAT
      NEMINI;
VIVE IN DIES ET HORAS, NAM PROPRIUM EST NIHIL.
SALVIUS ET HEROS DANT.

CIL 1,2,1219

These are the bones of Pompeia's eldest daughter
Fortune promises much to many, but grants it to none.
Live for the day and the hour, for nothing is our own.
Salvius and Eros erected this stone.

The probable date of this inscription is the late second or early first century B.C.E.
Some editors omit *multa* in l. 2. Cf. Martial's Epigram 12.10: *Fortuna multis det
nimis, satis nulli.*

l. 1 *ossua = ossa, heic = haec,* not *hic*

PLATE 13 (*RGM 331*)

Severina nutrix.
Date: Second half of the third century.

HOW IT SHOULD BE

Rome

DISCE QUISQUE PIUS PATER ES VEL MATER QUE GENERASTI:
NATOS HABERE BONU EST, SI NON SINT INVIDA FATA.
SIC TIBI NON RAPIAT MORS INVIDA TAM CITO NATOS,
UT MEIS ATQUE TUIS DIGNIS LEVE TERRA PRECERIS.
UT MORS IN VOLTUM VIVAT SEMPERQUE COLATUR   5
AELIUS MARCELLINUS PATER FILIO FELICISSIMO
HOC EGO FECI BENE, SI QUID SAPIUNT INFERI.

CE 647

Learn this,
Whoever you are,
A worthy father
Or perchance a mother
Who has born children,
To have offspring
Is a good thing
If only there were no jealous fates,
For then invidious death
Would not carry off
Your children so swiftly,
Compelling you to beg
The earth to rest lightly
Upon your children and mine,
Who deserve such treatment, and
So that death must
Seem a living being
Before our faces, requiring
Worship always.

I, Aelius Marcellinus his father,
Have made this well
For my son Felicissimus
If those below
Are wise.

This inscription, despite its clear and moving passages, poses many challenges. Note the disappearance of the final consonant (*-m*) in *bonu est* (line 2). The first four lines are addressed to *quisquis es*; then the subject shifts to *mors*. Death, of course, was not individually worshipped as a Roman deity, although Pluto, king of the underworld, was one of the Roman pantheon. *Mors . . . semperque colatur* (line 5) could therefore be translated as "requiring homage always," although this does not adequately explain the shift in emphasis, nor does it tell us how Death must be honored. Line 7 also poses problems. Are the *inferi* the inhabitants of Hades? What does their knowledge add to the fate of Felicissimus? My attempted solution is admittedly provisional.

THE EPITAPH OF QUINTUS ENNIUS

Rome, c. 163 B.C.E.

ASPICITE O CIVES, SENIS ENNI IMAGINIS FORMAM.
HIC VESTRUM PANXIT MAXIMA FACTA PATRUM.
NEMO ME DECORET DACRUNIS FUNERA FLETU FAXIT.
CUR? VOLITO VIVOS PER ORA VIRUM.

Ennius, Epigrams, I

Behold, citizens, this portrait of Ennius as an old man,
He who told the story of the greatest deeds of your fathers.
Let no one adorn my tomb
with tears. Why?
Because I flit about alive through
the mouths of men.

Quintus Ennius was the first important Roman poet. Although none of his works has survived in its entirety, he was widely quoted by later writers, including Cicero, who twice referred to the first line of this epitaph (*Tusc. Disp.* I 15, 34 and *Cato Maior* 20,73) . Note in line four the archaic spelling of *vivos* (in classical Latin, *vivus*). The meter is dactylic hexameter, in conscious imitation of Greek examples. The complete epigram appears in *Ennianae Poesis Reliquiae*. Recensit Ioannes Vahlen. Lipsiae: Teubneri, 1854, 162.

l. 3 *dacrunis* = *lacrymis* (cf. Greek δάκρυον), *faxit* = *faciat*

l. 4 *virum* = *virorum*

GOLDEN TONGUE

Rome

D ⊘ M
PARVVLVS HIC SITVS EST VIXIT TRIS VSQVE PER ANNOS
INQVE NOVEM MENSES INVALIDOSQ· DIES
NOMINE GRVSOGLOSVS AMABILIS VTQVE ERAT INFANS
5 FLEBILIS ET MISERE RAPTVS AD INFERIAS
SATVRNINVS · FILIO · VELIA · LALEMA
DELICATO · SVO · POSVIT

PARVULUS HIC SITUS EST. VIXIT TRIS USQUE PER ANNOS
INQUE NOVEM MENSES INVALIDOSQ(UE) DIES
NOMINE [CH]RUSOGLOS(S)US, AMABILIS, UTQUE ERAT INFANS
FLEBILIS ET MISERE RAPTUS AD INFERIAS.

CIL 6,14786

A little child lies here.
He lived three whole years, and into the ninth month
When days of illness struck him.
His name was Chrusoglossus and we loved him.
While still a child he was
borne with tears and sorrow
To the nether world.

While vocabulary and orthography pose no problems here, some expansion of these lines was necessary to bring out the full meaning of the Latin. Chrusoglossus lived *into* a ninth month after living *through* three years; whether the *invalidos dies* (l. 2) were part of the ninth month is not clear. The transfer of the meaning of *invalidos* from the span of time to the person preserves the meaning, if not the grammar, of the original. Likewise *amabilis* (l. 3) and *flebilis* (l. 4) are rendered as noun phrases.

A NONBELIEVER'S TOMB

Rome (Third Century C.E.?)

D. M. CERELIAE FORTUNATAE CONIUGI CARISSIMAE, CUM QUA V(IXI)
ANN(IS) XI S(INE) U(LLA) Q(UERELLA)...

Μή μου παρέλθῃς τὸ ἐπίγραμμα, ὁδοιπόρε,
ἀλλὰ σταθεὶς ἄκουε καὶ μαθὼν ἄπι·
οὐκ ἔστι ἐν Ἅδου πλοῖον, οὐ πορθμεὺς Χάρων,
οὐκ Αἴακος κλειδοῦχος, οὐχὶ Κέρβερος κύων·
ἡμεῖς δὲ πάντες οἱ κάτω τεθνηκότες   5
ὀστέα, τέφρα γεγόναμεν, ἄλλο δὲ οὐδὲ ἕν.
εἴρηκα σοι ὀρθῶς· ὕπαγε, ὁδοιπόρε,
μὴ καὶ τεθνακὼς ἀδ[ό]λεσχός σοι φανῶ.

To the shade of Cerelia Fortunata, my most precious wife, with whom
for eleven years I lived without a single quarrel...

Do not pass by my epitaph,
Wayfarer, but when you have
stopped, hear and learn,
then depart.
There is no boat
To carry you to Hades,
No ferryman Charon,
No judge Aeacus, no
Dog Cerberus.
All of us below
Have become bones and ashes.
Truly, I have nothing more to tell you,
So depart, wayfarer,
Lest dead though I am
I seem to you a teller of vain tales.

Do not favor this monument with sweet smelling oils, or garlands
It is but a stone.

Do not feed the funeral flames
It is a waste of money.

If you can give, give while I live.
Pouring wine on the ashes
Will only turn them to mud
And the dead will not drink.

For so I shall be.
And when you have heaped up earth on these remains
Say that what this was, it will never be again.

EG 646

This inscription is a personal favorite. One wonders how widespread the sentiments expressed were, nor is it clear whether these attitudes are those of the deceased or of the writer, if he was someone else. The only significant liberty taken with the translation is rendering ἐν Ἅδου as "to carry you to Hades." Although this inscription is reported to be dificult to read, paleographic evidence points to a date in the late empire.

ABOUT THE TRANSLATOR

Paul Shore studied classics at Lewis and Clark College, and at Yale University, where he earned an M.A. in history. He received his Ph.D. in Foundations of Education from Stanford University. He is currently an Associate Professor of Education at Saint Louis University, St. Louis, Missouri. His other books include *Awakening the Inner Eye: Intuition in Education*, with Nel Noddings (New York: Teachers College Press, 1984); *Encounters, Estrangements, Connections* (Moorhead, MN: Dacotah Territory Press, 1989); *The Myth of the University* (Lanham, MD: University Press of America, 1992); and *Seasons of Change: Reflections on Fifty Years at Saint Louis University* with Paul C. Reinert, S.J. (St. Louis: St. Louis University Press, 1996). He first became interested in classical tomb inscriptions while visiting the Römisch-Germanisches Museum in Cologne, Germany, as an undergraduate.

OTHER TITLES FROM
BOLCHAZY-CARDUCCI PUBLISHERS, INC.

Vergil's Dido and Mimus Magicus (CD with 40-page libretto in Latin, English, and German), composed by Jan Novák, conducted by Rafael Kubelik.
1997, ISBN 086516-346-4

Latin Music Through the Ages (cassette and book), by Cynthia Kaldis.
Book: 1991, paperback, ISBN 0-86516-242-5
Cassette: 1991, ISBN 0-86516-249-2

The Confessions of St. Augustine: Selections from Books I-IX, ed. by J.M. Campbell and M.R.P. McGuire.
1984 (reprint of 1931), paperback, ISBN 0-86516-058-9

On Unbelievable Tales: Palaephatus Peri Apiston, ed. by Jacob Stern.
1996, hardbound, ISBN 0-86516-310-3
1996, paperback, ISBN 0-86516-320-0

Fides Quaerens Intellectum, by S.J. Tester.
1989, paperback, ISBN 086516-221-2

Millennium: A Latin Reader, A.D. 374-1374, by F.E. Harrison.
1991 (reprint of 1968), paperback, ISBN 0-86516-191-7

Bede's Historia Ecclesiastica, by F.W. Garforth.
1988 (reprint of 1988), paperback, ISBN 0-86516-218-2

Jesuit Latin Poets of the 17th and 18th Centuries, selected and paraphrased by James J. Mertz, John P. Murphy, with Jozef IJsewijn.
1989, hardbound, ISBN 0-86516-214-X
1989, paperback, ISBN 0-86516-215-8

The Meaning of "Baptism," by James W. Dale.
Classic Baptism, 1989 (reprint of 1867), paperback, ISBN 0-86516-224-7
Judaic Baptism, 1991 (reprint of 1869), paperback, ISBN 0-86516-247-6
Johannic Baptism, 1993 (reprint of 1871), paperback, ISBN 0-86516-259-X
Christic and Patristic Baptism, 1995 (reprint of 1874), paperback, ISBN 0-86516-263-8